STUDIES IN
THE BOOK OF DEUTERONOMY דברים
THE RENEWAL OF THE COVENANT

Book 2: Deuteronomy 11:26–26:15

Ariel Berkowitz

Shoreshim Publishing
71040 Memphis Ridge Rd.
Richmond, Michigan 48062
Phone: 586-588-0193
Email: ad.tri@mac.com
www.torahtruths.com

DEDICATION

Since producing Book 1, we experienced the sudden and sorrowful passing of a close dear friend and colleague:

Dr. David Friedman ז״ל

It is to him that we wish to dedicate this
entire Deuteronomy study series.

David was mighty in Torah — both the Living and the Written. His heart and mind were also dedicated to teaching, both in Israel and internationally. Most of all, David was not only a biblical scholar, but a kind and warm-hearted husband, father, grandfather, and friend.

Just like the Holy One said to Moshe, so it also applies to David:
"For it is not an idle Word for you; indeed, it is your life.
And by this Word you will prolong your days in the Land..."
(Deuteronomy 32:47)

כי לוא-דבר רק הוא מכם"

כי-הוא חייכם ובדבר

הזה תארִַכו ימים על-האדמה ..." "

The Torah was David's life. He spent his days living in the Land, working to defend the Land, and helping many others to love God's Land.

Acknowledgments

Those who have Book 1 of this series on Deuteronomy will notice that the acknowledgements in this book are almost the same. That is because there has been little change in helpers from Book 1 to Book 2. Neither do we anticipate any change for the forthcoming final book!

Much appreciation goes to our good friend, Hugo Buitenhuis of Aalsmeer, Netherlands for spending some of his retirement days by painstakingly laying this book out into the format in which it now is. Our daughter, Rachel also assisted, especially in Books 2 and 3. In Books 2 and 3, we want to acknowledge our skillful and graceful editors from the UK: Dr. Winnie Chen and Dolly Salins. We thank Jim Xavier of Kent, Washington for making our meager design into a beautiful cover for this booklet. Last, but certainly not least, I lovingly thank my wife and colleague, D'vorah, for encouraging this project and helping to provide the time necessary to complete it and other such works.

PREFACE

A MUST TO READ!

This book is not intended to be a thorough verse-by-verse exegesis of the Book of Deuteronomy. Accordingly, many passages from the biblical text are not included in this study and various concepts are not covered either. Furthermore, we have tried to keep footnotes to a minimum. A bibliography of the main sources is included at the end. The reason for this brevity is so the student will gain a thorough overview of the Book of Deuteronomy without getting bogged down in many details.

In addition, the student will notice that we have chosen to use the question-and-answer method to study Deuteronomy. The engaging questions are based on the text of the New American Standard Bible. However, some questions or quotations, are based on our own translation from the original Hebrew, which we will clarify when needed.

While there is an abundance of questions for each chapter, which the student is encouraged to answer by filling in the blanks, we have also provided essential comments, linguistic explanations, and other background information to help the student understand the text better and to assist him/her in answering the questions.

Next, please note how we mark dates. We will not use the customary western way of dating: BC for "**B**efore **C**hrist" and AD for After Christ ("**A**nno **D**omini"). Instead, we will use a traditional Jewish method of dating: BCE (**B**efore the **C**ommon **E**ra) and CE (**C**ommon **E**ra).

Note that we are referring to what Christians call "The Old Testament" as the "Tanakh" (תנ"ך). This is an acronym meaning:

T – Torah (תורה)
N – Nevi'im (נביאים) or Prophets
Kh – Ketuvim (כתובים) or Writings

The term Tanakh represents the traditional Jewish three-fold division of the Hebrew Scriptures. This way of dividing the Scriptures was used even before the time of Yeshua. Yet, Yeshua did not use the term "Tanakh." It was coined centuries after Him. However, He did acknowledge and use the traditional three-fold division. See, for example Luke 24:27, 44. The term Tanakh is more helpful in that it bypasses the often-misunderstood term Old Testament.

We will refer to the New Testament as the Apostolic Scriptures or the Greek Scriptures, removing the often-misunderstood term New Testament. When many people read "Old Testament" they often erroneously think that this part of the Bible is out of date and, therefore, not relevant for us today. Similarly, when people read "New Testament" they sometimes think that it is what has replaced the antiquated Old Testament. We do not want to propagate those ways of thinking about the Bible. Hence, we will consistently employ the terms "Tanakh" and "Apostolic Scriptures" (or Greek Scriptures).

Finally, we have chosen to use the names "Yeshua" instead of "Jesus," "Moshe" in place of "Moses," and "Messiah" rather than the title "Christ." These substitutions we believe, add to the Hebraic character of our study and help in a small way to remind us that we are commenting on a book from the Hebrew Scriptures.

More Abbreviations

Please note the following frequent abbreviations used in this booklet:

ANE	The Ancient Near East
BDB	Brown, Driver, and Briggs Hebrew Lexicon
EBC	Expositor's Bible Commentary
HALOT	Koehler and Baumgartner, *Hebrew and Aramaic Lexicon of the Old Testament*
JPS	Jewish Publication Society
LXX	The Septuagint
NASB	New American Standard Bible
MT	Masoretic Text (Hebrew)
NET	New English Translation Notes
TOTC	Tyndale Old Testament Commentary

Objectives

This booklet series is intended as a self-study on the biblical Book of Deuteronomy. It is designed for the student to think through the entire Book of Deuteronomy at his/her own pace. The main objective is to explore Deuteronomy section by section by reading the biblical text and answering the questions we have provided. Along the way, we have emphasized key passages, maps to peruse, and pictures that will help to elucidate the passages under investigation.

We wrote this booklet with several other objectives in mind. First, to facilitate the earnest Bible student to become more familiar with the contents and flow of thought of the Book of Deuteronomy. Second, to help the student see how Deuteronomy provides the basis for life in the Land of Israel. However, note that although Deuteronomy first and foremost applies to ancient Israel living in the Land of Promise, we believe that the instructions contained in the Torah apply to all generations of Israelites who reside there, including the Israelis living there today. A third objective is to give the student a glimpse of how meaningful and practical this fifth book of Moses is for the corporate life of all of God's redeemed people, no matter where they live. Finally, we want to help the student gain a better understanding of the Holy One as a God who is in covenant relationship with His chosen people.

Note:

Deuteronomy is a long book! Because of that we have divided our study of it into three parts, which will make three books:

Book 1 — Deuteronomy 1:1–11:25
Book 2 — Deuteronomy 11:26–26:15
Book 3 — Deuteronomy 26:16–34:12

This present volume is Book 2 — Deuteronomy 11:26–26:15

The Organization of This Book

As explained in the first book of this series in Deuteronomy, we are exploring Deuteronomy according to its similarities with a typical 13th–15th century BCE Hittite Suzerain/Vassal Treaty.

In the chart below we have compared the flow of thought for Deuteronomy with a typical Hittite Suzerain/Vassal Treaty. We are basing our outline of Deuteronomy on this comparison. Moreover, this outline will also serve as an outline for these study books. This type of outline also provides us with the correct perspective with which to interpret Deuteronomy. Knowing this covenantal structure also has tremendous implications for our understanding of the entire document of Torah.

HITTITE TREATY	DEUTERONOMY
Preamble	1:1–6
Historical Prologue	1:7–4:49
Stipulations	5:1–26:15
Blessings and Problems	26:16–30:20
Witnesses	30:19
Covenant Continuity and Renewal	31
Covenant Reminder	32

Based on this comparison, we are proposing the following outline for the Book of Deuteronomy.

I.	Preamble: Covenant Mediator	1:1–5
II.	Historical Prologue: Covenant History	1:6–4:49
III.	Covenant Responsibilities:	5:1–26:15
IV.	Covenant Conditions and Ratification	26:16–30:20
V.	Covenant Continuity	31:1–34:12

This work (Book 2) in our *Studies in Deuteronomy,* begins in the midst of point number III above: "Covenant Responsibilities." As we can see, this section of Deuteronomy is very long, comprising the bulk of the book. Accordingly, we have divided the Covenant Responsibilities into two main sections. We studied the first part in Book 1. We saw that it emphasized the "unseen instructions," such as love, hearing God, or remembering Him and His Word. Hence, we finished Book 1 at the end of Deuteronomy Chapter 11.

Beginning near the end of Chapter 11, Deuteronomy begins to teach us how to live holy lives — separated unto the Lord — in just about every area of life. That is how we will approach our study of this section of Deuteronomy. We will go through the chapters exploring what they say about holy living, topic by topic — as the text unfolds these in Book 1, we neglected to mention an alternative way of reading through and studying Deuteronomy.

Jewish people have been reading the Five Books of Moses (The Torah) seemingly since time immemorial! Some communities read through the entire Torah systematically in a three-year cycle, others use a 1-year reading cycle. In order to facilitate the reading, the entire Torah has been divided into smaller portions where a fixed amount of material is read publicly in the synagogue and studied each week. These smaller portions were determined centuries ago. They even have names! Each weekly portion (Hebrew: *parasha,* פרשה pl.: *parashiyot,* פרשיות) is named after the first important Hebrew word in the text. For centuries most communities have used the 1-year cycle (though not exclusively). This cycle goes from October, at the end of Sukkot, to the next conclusion of Sukkot.

Look at the following chart to see the names of the parashiyot (Torah Portions) of Deuteronomy and the verses they cover.

Torah Portion	Content of the Torah Portion
Devarim	Deuteronomy 1:1–3:22
Vaetchanan	Deuteronomy 3:23–7:11
Ekev	Deuteronomy 7:12–11:25
Re'eh	Deuteronomy 11:26–16:17
Shoftim	Deuteronomy 16:18–21:9
Ki Tetze	Deuteronomy 21:10–25:19
Ki Tavo	Deuteronomy 26:1–29:8
Nitsavim	Deuteronomy 29:9–30:20
Vayelekh	Deuteronomy 31:1–30
Ha'azinu	Deuteronomy 32:1–52
Vezo't Ha-b'rakhah	Deuteronomy 33:1–34:12

In essence, we have covered the first three parashiyot in Book 1: Devarim, Vaetchanan, and Ekev. Book 2 will cover Re'eh, Shoftim, and Ki Tetze. Then in Book 3 we will finish the book with the final 5 parashiyot (some of them are short).

Having explained the nature of the organization of this, Book 2, we are now ready to dive into our studies.

THE COVENANT RENEWAL: 11:26–32

Our study begins with a short review of the context of our passages in Deuteronomy. This context is in Deuteronomy 11:26–32. The entire book of Deuteronomy is a renewal of the covenant God made with Israel on Mt. Sinai after the Holy One brought us out of slavery in Egypt. The Israelites, 40 years later, are now on the east bank of the Jordan River, at the foot of the mountains of Moab. Look at the map below and focus on the center of the map, just north of the Dead Sea. There they are receiving final instructions from Moshe before they cross the river and begin the conquest of the Land. Included in those final instructions and the renewal of the covenant of Mt. Sinai, in 11:26–32, Moshe teaches them to renew this covenant once again. The following questions focus on that covenant renewal.

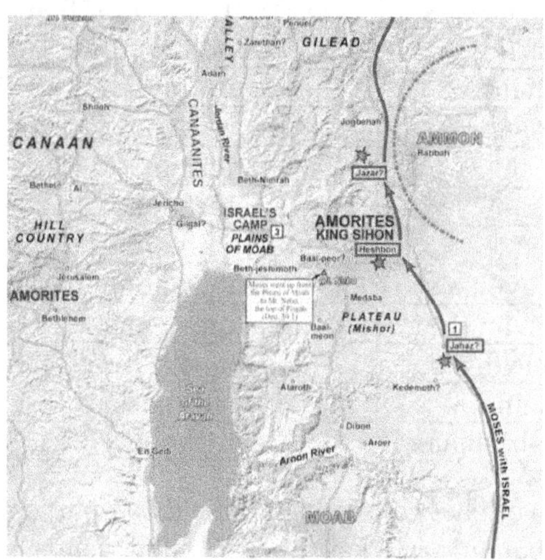

Map 1-Location of the Israelites in the Book of Deuteronomy

1. What were the Israelites instructed to do when they cross the Jordan and enter the Land? (11:29–32)

____

____

2. What is significant about the location? (See Genesis 12:6)

____

____

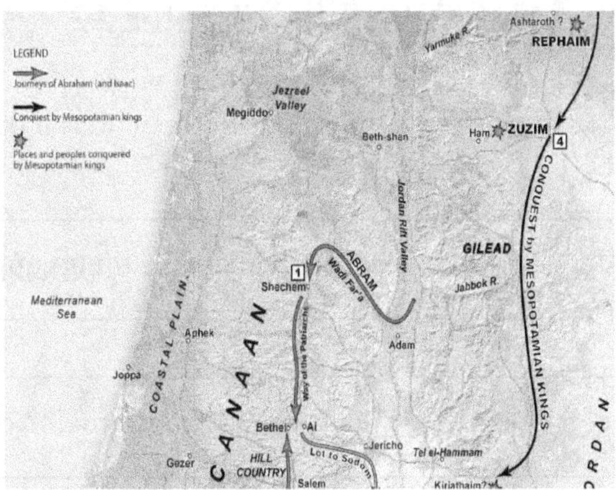

Map 2-Abraham Entering the Land of Canaan

This map above shows the route Abraham took to enter the Land of Canaan. It was also the same route that Jacob used to re-enter the Land after his sojourn with Laban. Notice where Shechem is, in the center of the map. It is also practically in the center of the Land of Israel! That is where God instructed Israel to renew the covenant once they began to conquer the Land under Joshua.

> In 11:28 we encounter the word "curse" in English. The Hebrew word is *qelalah* (קללה). It has to do with being insignificant. In other words, if Israel was not faithful to the covenant, God would treat them as if they are insignificant. They are not; but it would look that way. This will be fleshed out later in Deuteronomy chapters 27–29.

3. Why do you think another covenant renewal was appropriate after Israel began the conquest of the Land?

____

____

Holy Worship: Chapter 12

1. How does Moshe describe the nature of the material he is about to discuss? (12:1)

   ____

2. According to 12:1, where especially do these things apply?

   ____

   ____

3. When Israel entered the Land, what were they to do?

   ____

   Why do you think the Lord instructed them to do these things?

   ____

   ____

4. According to 12:4–11, where was Israel instructed to worship their God?

   ____

5. What are two uses of animals for the Israelites according to this passage? (12:6–7 and 12:15, 20)

   ____

   ____

   ____

   How can we discern that the text is speaking about two different uses of animals? (12:15)

   ____

   ____

6. What was one thing Israel was not allowed to eat? (12:16, 23–25)

   ____

   Why do you think this is so?

   ____

   ____

Does this only apply to Israelites, or does it apply to others? Explain your answer.

7. How does the Lord describe their attitude toward worshipping Him, especially when they bring Him offerings, tithes, etc.? (12:7, 12, 18)

8. In Map 3, the black lines represent major trade routes and military roads in the ANE. Look at the map and try to determine what is the strategic importance of this location in God's plan.

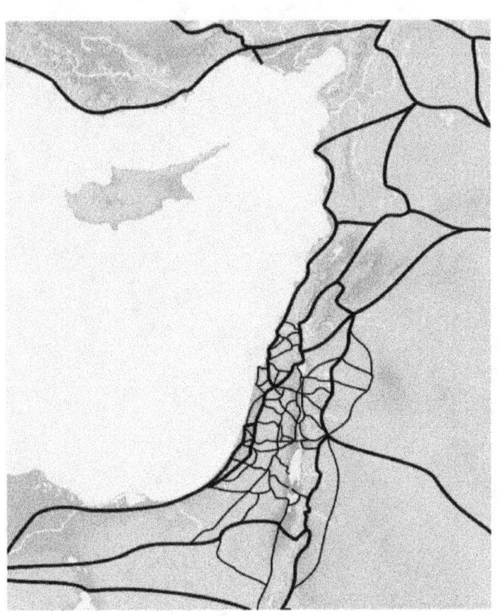

Map 3-Major transportation routes in the ANE[1]

9. What does Moshe warn the Israelites in 12:28–32?

---

[1] This map was made using the Atlas application in Accordance Bible Software.

10. What application, if any, does this have for all believers today?

____

____

____

11. In 12:32 we see a repetition of what Moshe taught in 4:2. What does Moshe tell us to be careful to do regarding the commandments?

____

____

Can you give some examples of how those instructions have been violated throughout history?

____

____

____

Holy Listening: Chapter 13

Chapter 13 deals with several possible ways by which the Israelites could have been enticed to become unfaithful to the Lord and seek other loyalties. Let us look at each possibility separately. Read through this chapter and glean from the verses what the passage (Chapter 13) says specifically how the Israelites could be enticed.

A False Prophet   13:1–5

1. What constitutes a false prophet?

2. According to 13:1–2, what are some of the things that a false prophet might do to entice others to follow what he/she says?

   What does this say about people who perform what they call "signs" and "wonders" today?

3. Why would the Lord permit such a one to come among them? (13:3)

4. What was to be done to such a false prophet and why? (13:5)

5. Since governments today do not allow believers to do these things to false prophets, what might believers do instead to false prophets?

"Trusted" Enticers 13:6–11

The second group of enticers appear to be those who we know, related to, and apparently trust.

1. What kinds of people does the text specify in this second
   group of enticers? (13:6)

____

____

2. According to 13:6–11 what does the text say to do with such people
   if they try to get the Israelites to forsake the Lord?

____

____

Unnamed Enticers from a Known City   13:12–18

The Hebrew text in 13:13 refers to this last group of enticers as *anashim b'nei beliyya'al* (אהשים בני בליעל). The question is, what specifically does this phrase mean? We checked several places. The best answer seems to come from the *JPS Torah Commentary* on Deuteronomy. Commentator Jeffrey H. Tigay writes:

> The precise meaning of *beliya'al* is uncertain. Various antisocial types are called *benei beliya'al*, such as murderers and rapists, false witnesses, rebels, corrupt priests, drunks, ingrates, boors, and the selfish. Many scholars think that *beliya'al* is a compound noun consisting of *beli*, "without," and a noun, *ya'al*, which refers to some positive quality such as value or honor. Thus, *benei beliya'al* may mean "useless" or "dishonorable" men. The question is complicated by the fact that *beliya'al* is also used as a term for death or the nether world, which calls for quite a different etymology, such as "(the land from which one) does not come up" (*bal ya'al*) or "the swallower" (from *b-l-ʿ*, "swallow"). This meaning is reflected in "Belial," a name of Satan in the Dead Sea Scrolls, the Pseudepigrapha, and the Christian Scriptures.
>
> The two meanings of *beliya'al* may be unrelated and they may be homonyms, but it is conceivable that the term originally meant "the nether world" and that *benei beliya'al* meant "denizens of the nether world" or "demons," and then "evildoers," "scoundrels."[2]

---

[2] Jeffrey H. Tigay, *The JPS Torah Commentary: Deuteronomy*, 134.

Whatever the term means, no matter how one looks at it, these are not good people! Yet they existed within Israel and had the potential to lure other Israelites away from faithfulness to the Lord.

1. According to 13:14, what is the first thing Israel was instructed to do with such enticers?

____

____

   a. What do you think about this process?

____

____

   b. What does this process teach us about God?

____

____

   c. What can this process teach us about conducting affairs in the body of Messiah?

____

____

2. If there are such evil enticers, what does the text tell us to do with the city from which they came?

____

____

Why do you think that the entire city disciplined and not just the individual who are leading people away from the Lord?

____

This chapter is focused primarily on what is considered to be food for God's people. We also learn a few other things brought into the discussion about food.

1. 14:1–2 mentions four expressions by which God's people are identified. What are they?

____

____

____

____

The Hebrew grammar of the verb in 14:3 seems like it is a command. However, it is not an imperative verb. It is either an imperfect or a participle. In other words, we can put the verb in our own words like this: "Knowing who you are (based on the information of 14:1–2), you are not a person who eats the kinds of things that the following verses mention. It is not part of your identity to do so!" (For that matter it is the same verbal construction in 14:1)

2. What do you think is the difference between saying: "You shall not_____________" and "You are not the kind of person who _______________."?

____

____

____

____

3. What is/are the reason(s) in the text for separating different kinds of living creatures into food and not food? (14:1–2)

____

____

____

4. Why do you think that the Torah places such an emphasis on what kinds of food we eat? (The hint is in 14:2)

A TRADITIONAL JEWISH PHILOSOPHY FOR EATING:

Moderation — Eat only what is needed, no gluttony.

Sanctification — Say a blessing to the Holy One before and after, to take a moment to think about what it is we are eating and from where it comes.

Celebration — Food is essential for celebrating life, fellowship, and special moments together with the Lord.

From *Blessing of a Skinned Knee* by Dr. Wendy Mogel

5. What characteristics must *animals* possess to be considered food? (14:4–8)

6. What characteristics must *water creatures* possess to be considered food? (14:9–10)

7. What characteristics must *birds* possess to be considered food? (14:11–20)

Excursus:
Does God Permit Us to Eat Cheeseburgers?

What kind of question is this in a Deuteronomy study book? Those who are Jewish understand from where we are coming. Deuteronomy 14:21 (as well as Exodus 23:19 and 34:26) contains an instruction that has become the basis for many Jewish people separating dairy foods/drinks from meat food (and even dairy utensils from meat utensils, etc. It reads: "You shall not boil a young goat in its mother's milk." We need to ask, 1) Do, in fact, these words teach us to separate meat from dairy? 2) Are there any other ways of understanding this verse and the parallel passages elsewhere in Torah?

Let us first look at the details of 14:21, then ask some questions about them. The first part of the question should be answered straight from the verse. The second part of the question is a "think" question. The answer is not too evident directly from the text.

1. What kind of animal is specified in 14:21?_________________
   - Why not another kind of animal, such as cows?

2. What is the method of cooking specified in14:21?__________
   - Why does the text specify "boiling" and not a different kind of cooking method?

3. In what was the kid not to be cooked? _________________
   - Why its mother's milk and not just any kind of milk?

It seems that a very specific issue 14:21 was being addressed, because the details seem to be very specific. If it was merely a general prohibition against eating meat and dairy products together, Moshe would have said it plainly, like so many of the other daily instructions in the Torah.

Let us be clear: We do not believe that separating milk from meat is a teaching from the Torah. Commentators have suggested at least two other possible ways of interpreting this verse.

1. An Instruction against Canaanite Religious Practices

Deuteronomy 14:1 begins the passage with an instruction against Israel doing Canaanite mourning practices. The conclusion of the passage (14:21) follows a list of what is considered food and not considered food. Thus, this injunction in 14:21 seems like it comes out of nowhere! Yet, keeping with the context, it might be possible that not boiling a kid in its mother's milk might be in conjunction with doing a Canaanite religious practice, perhaps even a mourning practice. In fact,

> the regular birth of goats near Sukkot (in the fall) and their inclusion in celebratory meals may be the basis of this law. It may also be based on an injunction to treat animals humanely, since an animal still nursing may have mother's milk in its stomach. There is also the consideration that mother's milk contains blood and would therefore corrupt either sacrificial meat or meals.[3]

Furthermore, historian Jack Finegan adds, "One rite mentioned in the Ras Shamra texts in which the seething of a kid in milk is prescribed as an item in the magical technique for producing early rains." This sounds very familiar with what Deuteronomy 14:21 prohibits about cooking a kid in its mother's milk.[4]

2. Bring in All of the First Fruits

This second possible interpretation comes from a very unlikely source. It is from a book about studying the Torah written by a prominent Jerusalem rabbi, Dr. Avigdor Bonchek. Bonchek, like so many other religious Jews, is part of a Jewish religious community that practices separating meat from dairy and uses this passage, as well as the ones from Exodus for biblical support!

Bonchek notes that the verb usually translated as "seethe" or "boil" (*bashal*, בשל) can have an entirely different connotation. It has been used in contexts which have to do with becoming ripe or becoming mature. Actually, the esteemed lexicon, HALOT agrees with this.[5] Giving this alternative understanding of the verb, Bonchek writes, "The phrase then means, 'Thou shall not allow a kid to become mature with its mother's milk, that is you should not allow the kid to mature, rather bring it as a sacrifice in the Temple'."[6] This understanding fits the context of Exodus which speaks about bringing in the First Fruit offerings.

Hence, if this interpretation is correct, Deuteronomy 14:21 is not

---

[3] John H. Walton, Victor H. Matthews and Mark W. Chavalas, *IVP Bible Background Commentary: Old Testament.* 103.

[4] Jack Finegan, *Light from the Ancient Past,* vol. 1, 174. Ras Shamra is a location on the Mediterranean coast in Syria. It is the modern name for ancient Ugarit, a coastal Canaanite city from which archaeologists have discovered a horde of clay tablets with inscriptions (ostraca) dated from close to the time of Moshe.

[5] HALOT, 164.

[6] Avigdor Bonchek, *Studying the Torah: A Guide to In-Depth Interpretation,* 55.

about separating meat from dairy. Rather, by rendering the verb bashal as "becoming ripe" or "mature," we can see that the verse is about bringing in the kid while it is still young as a First Fruit offering and do not let it mature by drinking its mother's milk.

We think this is a very reasonable explanation. What does the reader think?

HOLY GIVING: 14:22–29

We are beginning to see that the Torah has instructions for how to live our daily lives. It covers just about every area of our lives and teaches us how to live holy lives, that is, how to live lives that are separated from the world and dedicated to serving the Holy One of Israel.

1. What is the context for the instructions about giving (14:22–29)?

2. What is to be tithed according to 14:22?

3. Where is the tithe to be brought? (14:23)

4. What is to be done with the tithe? (14:23)

5. What is the reason for this, according to 14:23?

    What do you think this means?

6. If someone lives too far away from the place to where the tithe should go, what are they permitted to do with the tithe? (14:24)

7. According to 14:24–26, who benefits from this tithe and what may they do with it?

8. Who else is to receive a tithe according to 14:27–29?

9. According to 14:22–29, approximately how much is the required giving among God's people?

HOLY FINANCING: 15:1–11

1. What does 15:1 instruct an Israeli to do?

____

____

How is this to be done? (15:2–3)

____

____

2. If the community practiced this, what might happen, according to 15:4–6?

____

____

3. How are the poor people to be treated in the 7th year in regard to their creditors? (15:7–11)

____

____

HOLY LAND: 15:12–18

The previous section was about financing. However, the previous section also brought up the subject of the Land.

1. Hence, according to 15:1–6 what must be done at the end of every seven years?

____

The Hebrew calls this year a "*Shmittah*, שמטה,"
or a *Shanat Shmittah*, "A Year of Release."

Servitude was an accepted fact of life in Israel, as it was everywhere in the ancient world. Israel had both indentured servants and full slaves. Both are termed *'eved*, עבד, "servant."

2. When release comes, what is the servant to be given?
    (15:12–14)

____

____

3. What is the reason for such kindness? (15:15–18)

____

____

4. According to 15:15–18, what happens if the servant does not want to
    leave?

____

____

Why do you think a servant might want to leave the master?

____

____

In effect, the bondslave is declaring his undying and lifelong loyalty
to his creditor. The scar (or even hole) — and possibly an earring —
in the earlobe would testify to the community that the slave had
surrendered independence and personal rights. This may be what
Paul had in mind when he said, "I bear on my body the marks of
Yeshua." (Galatians 6:17)

5. How does Deuteronomy address the master's feelings about
    releasing a faithful servant? (15:18)

____

____

Reserving the Firstborn   15:19–23

1. According to 15:19 To whom does the firstborn male among the
    animals belong?

____

2. What shall be done with the firstborn male of one's animals? (15:20)

    a. ____

    b. ____

    c. ____

3. What should be done with the animals who have injuries or blemishes? (15:21)

____

____

4. What is not to be eaten/drunk? (15:22) _______________________

Holy Days: 16:1–17

The first part of chapter 16 teaches about the biblical holy days. The Torah has two names for these special calendar days. The first is *mo'ed*, מועד (pl. *mo'adim*, מועדים). The word mo'ed means an appointed time. This is what they are called in Leviticus 23. The second name is *hag*[7], חג (pl. *haggim*, חגים). A hag is a pilgrimage festival. They are first mentioned in Exodus 23. The main themes of these festivals are commemoration of the Exodus and gratitude for the harvest, thus teaching appreciation for the Land. We should note that all the haggim are also mo'adim, but not all mo'adim are haggim.

Hag (חג) – Exodus 23	Mo'ed (מועד) – Leviticus 23
	Shabbat
Pesach/Festival of Matza	Pesach/Festival of Matza
	First Fruit (Barley)
	The Counting Period
Shavuot	Shavuot
	Festival of Trumpets (New Year)
	Yom Kippur
Sukkot/The 8th Day	Sukkot/The 8th Day

---

[7] We have chosen to spell the Hebrew word חג as hag. Technically it should be rendered as chag. However, those who do not know Hebrew might be tempted to pronounce the ch in chag as a ch in the word <u>Charles</u>. Biblical Hebrew does not have such a sound. To avoid this, we are writing this word with an h instead of ch.

The chart above shows a list of the haggim and the mo'adim. Notice the biblical locations of each and that three of the mo'adim also are haggim. Deuteronomy 6 discusses specifically the haggim. Deuteronomy's purpose in mentioning them is to make the point that they must be observed at the chosen sanctuary. Hence, Moses continues his emphasis on having a central place for the tribes to gather where they would meet with the Lord. Let us examine one hag at a time as we go through this chapter.

Pesach (Passover) 16:1–8

1. Compare 16:1 with 16:16. What two names does the text give to Pesach? ____

   Why do you think these names are interchangeable?

   ____

   ____

2. On which date and time is Pesach to be celebrated? (16:1, 6)

   ____

3. What is the purpose of celebrating Pesach? (16:3)

   ____

4. Where is the Pesach offering to be sacrificed? (16:2)

   ____

5. How long is Pesach/Unleavened Bread to be celebrated? (16:8)

   ____

   Historically, why do you think it lasts for one week? In other words, what historical event is being remembered?

   ____

   ____

6. How is the final day to be celebrated? (16:8)

   ____

   ____

   What do you think is to be the emotional attitude for this season? Why?

   ____

   ____

According to the Hebrew of Deuteronomy 16:3 the bread eaten during Pesach/Festival of Unleavened bread is referred to by 3 names:

- Hametz (חמץ) – "Sour," or "Bitter"
- Matzah (מצה) – "Drained Out" (It is only made from flour and water; all other ingredients are left out.)
- Lechem 'Oni (לחם עוני) — Bread of Poverty, or Affliction

7. The words the Hebrew text uses to refer to the bread eaten at Pesach are listed in the box above. What do you think each of the names can tell us about the historical events they celebrated at Pesach/Unleavened Bread?

Hametz

____

____

Matzah

____

____

Bread of Poverty/Affliction

____

____

Shavuot 16:9–12

1. The name Shavuot means "Weeks." This hag lasts for one day. According to 16:9, how many weeks between Pesach and Shavuot?

____

2. What kind of offering is to be brought before the Lord at Shavuot? 16:10 _______________________________________

3. According to 16:11 what is to be the emotional attitude for this season? Why?

____

Sukkot   16:13–15

1. The name "Sukkot" means "booths" or "temporary shelters." Hence, the English name for this Festival is "Festival of Tabernacles." According to Leviticus 23, Sukkot begins on the 15th of the 7th month. According to Deuteronomy 16:13, for how long is Sukkot celebrated?

____

2. According to 16:13, after what events does Sukkot begin? What might that tell us about the nature of the festival?

____

3. Who is to be included in the celebrations at Sukkot? (16:14)

____

____

4. According to 16:15 what is to be the emotional attitude for this season? Why? (Look at the verse!)

____

____

5. 16:16–17 functions mainly as a kind of summary for the 3 haggim. When the Israelites appear before the Lord at these festivals, what are they to bring?

____

____

The Torah says much more about the festival days, especially in Leviticus 23 and Exodus 23. However, that is beyond our purpose and scope here in Deuteronomy. The student is encouraged to study these passages.

Dates in the Bible are often difficult to understand. On the next page is a chart summarizing the months in which these festivals take place. Some of the months in the Bible are mentioned by their Canaanite (or Hebrew?) title and others are mentioned by their Babylonian name, which Israel acquired during their Babylonian captivity.

Babylonian/Modern Name	Ancient Israelite or /Canaanite Name	Modern Equivalent
Nisan ניסן Nehemiah 2:1	Aviv אביב Exodus 13:4	March/April
Iyyar אייר	Ziv זיו 1 Kings 6:1	April/May
Sivan סיון Esther 8:9		May/June
Tammuz תמוז		June/July
Av אב		July/August
Elul אלול Nehemiah 6:15		August/September
Tishrei תשרי	Etanim אתנים 1 Kings 8:2	September/October
Bul בול 1 Kings 6:38	חשון Cheshvan	October/November
Kislev כסלו Nehemiah 1:1		November/December
	Tevet טבת Esther 2:16	December/January
	Shevat שבט Zechariah 1:7	January/February
	Adar אדר Esther 3:7	February/March
	Adar II אדר ב.	March

Between Chapters 16 to 20, Deuteronomy teaches about the national or Israelite governmental institutions. (There might be one or two diversions). We are surprised to learn that both the Priests and the Prophets are included in this list. This might indicate that, while Israel was to have a king, yet the Word of God and the Service of God are central to the character of the nation. These institutions are:

- The Courts
- The Priest
- The King
- The Prophet
- The Military

HOLY JUSTICE: 16:18–17:13

It is helpful to understand Deuteronomy chapters 12–26 to be elaborations of the 10 Words (The "Ten Commandments. In chapters 12–26, Moses is taking the Israelites through a transition from being a patriarchal, family-oriented society which they were in Egypt to a village-centered community structure which will be their situation in the Land — until they have a king. One of the major differences between those two kinds of societies is how justice is performed. That is the focus in this section.

1. Once they were living in the Land, what was Israel to appoint? (16:18)

____

2. Where does 16:18 say that these officials shall meet?

____

   In ancient Israel, the town court met at the city/village gate. Most gates had 4 to 6 chambers with the entrance road splitting them in half. Since most towns had one entrance gate (there were some exceptions, but few) it was natural for the city officials to meet at the gate in one of the chambers to control who enters and to conduct town business. A good example is in Ruth 4:1–12.

The picture above is the entrance gate at Tel Arad in southern Israel. It is from the Divided Kingdom period. Though Tel Arad functioned as a fort, helping to protect Judah's southern border, nevertheless the installation housed soldiers and their families. The men are pictured at the city gate, with the chambers on both sides of them. This is where the city court would have been.

3. List some of the characteristics of biblical justice in 16:19.

    a. ____

    b. ____

4. How is a case to be conducted according to 17:4?

    ____

    What do you think this means in practical terms?

    ____

5. Which kind of punishment is permitted according to 17:5?

    ____

    What is the purpose for permitting this kind of punishment? 17:7

    ____

    What are the roles of witnesses in such a situation?

    ____

6. What does the Torah say to do if the case is too difficult for the local judges? 17:8

    ____

7. According to 17:9, who were to be the judges if the case was taken
   to the next level?

8. If the person is found guilty, what were they required to do?
   (17:10–12)

9. What would happen if they did not do as told by the judges? Why?
   (17:12)

HOLY KINGS: 17:14–20

The next section of Deuteronomy discusses the national leadership of
Israel. Accordingly, it includes information about the kings, the
priesthood, the prophets, and finally the army.

Once again, it is significant that the national institutions include both
prophets and priests. This is an indication that although Israel would
eventually have a king, nevertheless, it was also to function as a
theocracy, as the Word of God and relationship to Him was paramount
and central to the nation.

Deuteronomy assumes that Israel will choose a king. It is not our
place here to discuss whether they *should have* a king or not, instead of
functioning as a pure theocracy. Deuteronomy merely provides the
principles by which a king of Israel shall function.

1. According to 17:14–15, who is to choose Israel's kings?

2. What was the nationality of the king supposed to be? (17:15)

   Why do you think that is so?

3. Why do you think the king should not multiply horses or wives?
   What does the text say? (17:16–17)

4. When the king sits on his throne (becomes a king) what does Moshe
   tell him to do and why? (17:18–20)

____

____

____

> In 17:18, when the English says that the king shall write a "copy
> of the Torah," the Hebrew uses the words, *mishneh haTorah*,
> משנה התורה. The word "mishneh" means "repitition." Later in
> Jewish history, about 200 years after Yeshua, the rabbis would
> write what is called "The Mishnah." This is the same word found
> here in 17:18. The Mishnah is oral instruction that has been
> transmitted from teacher to student by means of repetition.

5. What do you think? When the king is instructed to write his copy of
   the Torah, does it mean to write all five books of Torah, or just
   Deuteronomy, or just this passage we are studying?

____

____

____

6. According to 17:20, how should his attitude be toward the Torah and
   what would be the result if he was faithful to it as a king?

____

____

____

HOLY PRIESTS: 18:1–8

Know the Terms!

It is easy to confuse the terms "Priests" and "Levites". Both words are
used in our passage. The first word to know is "Levi" (לוי). This is the
name of one of the sons of Jacob by Leah. In time, like all the sons of
Jacob, Levi also became the name for one of the tribes as they grew in
number. Eventually, the Lord chose the tribe of Levi to be the one from
which the attendants and caretakers of the Tabernacle/Temple would
come.

The next word is "Levites" (לוים) As the name sounds, these are the descendants of Levi. However, in our passage, as well as in many other places in the Scriptures, the Levites were designated to assist the sons of Aaron in the Temple service, being in charge of the furniture and utensils, the flour, wine, oil, incense, and spices — everything required for the service. Later in Israelite history, they also served as gatekeepers to the Temple complex, collectors of the Temple taxes, and even as singers in the choir that sung in the daily Temple services.

Finally, we have the term "priests" (*cohenim*, כוהנים). They were distinguished from other descendants by their genealogy. The cohenim were descendants of Levi, his son Kohat, and then through Aaron.

> The priest was essentially the guardian of the holy place.... To do this he took on the holiness of the sanctuary. This invested him with a kind of authority, but responsibility also. He had to bear the guilt for any lapse of propriety in the sanctuary.... Though all the people were to follow the Torah and are commanded to be holy..., the priests were the paradigm holy people...The *kōhēn's* liturgical functions were first and foremost to preside over the many types of sacrifice at the main altar... .[8]

One of the basic theological principles of ancient Israel was that they were in a covenantal relationship with their God. Since their God was viewed as being holy, the people were also to be holy. The corporate responsibility of maintaining the unique relationship with God was vested in prophet, priest, and king.

1. What does 18:1 say about the tribal inheritance for the descendants of Levi?

   ____

   ____

   Why do you think it was that way?

   ____

   ____

---

[8] David Noel Freedman, Editor-in-Chief, *Eerdmans Dictionary of the Bible*, 1082.

2. According to 18:1 and 3, what was to be a major food source for the Levites and Priests?

____

3. Which specific portions of the animals would be theirs?

____

____

4. What do you think it means when we are told that the "Lord is their inheritance, "in 18:2?

____

____

5. Keeping in mind what we wrote above concerning the basic functions of the priests, what do you think is means in 18:5 when we are told that they are "to stand and serve in the name of the Lord forever?"

____

____

6. In summary, who is to supply the basic support for the priests and Levites in their work?

____

____

HOLY PROPHETS: 18:9–22

1. It would be good to review Deuteronomy 13:1–5 which teaches about prophets. Why do you think Moshe might have divided his instructions about prophets into two sections, Chapter 13 and here in chapter 18?

____

____

2. Why do you think that Moshe prefaces his instructions about prophets with a reminder to avoid being like the Canaanites in 18:9–14?

____

3. What eight specific Canaanite practices are mentioned in 18:9–14?

4. What does the Lord think about such practices according to 18:11–12?

5. What does God promise to provide for His people according to 18:18?

Note: It might be helpful to remember the basic meaning of the Hebrew term for "prophet." It is *navi* (נביא) and it means "to bring." Hence, biblically speaking, the primary function of a prophet is to bring God's words to people.

6. Compare this definition above with what 18:18 says.

7. Under what circumstances should someone listen to the words of the prophet? (18:19)

8. If someone does not listen to the words of a prophet sent by God, what will happen to him/her? (18:19)

Note: When 18:19 says in the NASB, "I myself will require it of him." The Hebrew word translated "require" emphasized that God will "make him answer for it"; or "will hold accountable." [9]

9. What is to happen to someone who says he/she is a prophet but does not speak in God's Name? 18:20

____

Note: When the NASB reads "presumptuously," the Hebrew word means, "to treat mischievously" or to "behave insolently."[10]

10. According to 18:20, it is possible for someone to claim he/she is a prophet but speak words which are not from God. How do you think we can guard ourselves from following such a false prophet?

____

____

____

11. What is the test that 18:20–22 mentions?

____

____

> The Holy One wants us to guard ourselves and not be fooled into following someone who claims to be a prophet, even though they might be speaking in the name of the Lord and performing what is called "signs" and "wonders." Prophets must be tested!

12. What should happen to the false prophet according to 18:20?

____

Since we do not have the authority to do that to someone today, what are some ways which we can carry out what 18:20 says?

____

____

---

[9] *The NET Bible*, Second Edition Notes, Notes on Deuteronomy 18:19.
[10] HALOT, 268.

13. What should our attitude be toward that false prophet?

____

Cities of Refuge: Chapter 19

1. How does God provide for someone who accidently kills another person? (19:1–3)

____

____

2. How does 19:4 further define such a manslayer?

____

____

3. Why does God tells the Israelites to set aside places for such a manslayer to flee? (19:5–6, 10)

____

____

> The cities were to have been in the main parts of the Land: Galilee, Samaria, Judah, Golan, Gilead, and a location unknown. This made it easier for an innocent one to flee his possible avenger. See Numbers 35:15 also.

Map 4-Cities of Refuge[11]

____

[11] This map was made using the Atlas application in Accordance Bible Software.

4. What would happen when the Israelites expand their borders? (19:8)

____

____

5. According to 19:6, why would the manslayer need to flee to a safe place to flee?

____

____

Numbers chapter 35 teaches us more about what to do with one who killed someone accidently. We think it is important to get the complete picture, so we are digressing a little from Deuteronomy to bring in Numbers 35.

1. According to Numbers 35:12, what was to happen to the manslayer once in the City of Refuge?

____

____

2. How long must someone live in the City of Refuge, once he/she flees there? (Numbers 35:25)

____

3. What warning does Numbers 35:26–27 give to the manslayer?

____

____

4 After the death of the High Priest, what must a person do? (Numbers 35:28)

____

5. Why do you think it must wait until after the High Priest dies?

____

____

More about the Cities of Refuge

- By connecting activity in the City of Refuge to the High Priest, the text might be suggesting that the cities of refuge were considered to be extensions of the Temple Altar, where one could go to plead for mercy.

- It further underscored the idea of the judicial importance of the priests and the central Altar.

- Banishment to the city of refuge itself was not construed as making atonement for the dead man's blood. Since the blood of the slain, although spilled accidentally, cannot be avenged through the death of the slayer, it is ransomed through the death of the High Priest, which releases all homicides from their cities of refuge.

Murder: 19:11–21   (Back to Deuteronomy!)

The Hebrew term translated "kill" (*rotzeach*, רוצח) means someone who has committed homicide either acting with premeditation, (meaning murderer) as in Numbers 35:16–21, 31; Deuteronomy 22:26, or acting without premeditation as in Numbers 35:6, 11, 25–28 and Deuteronomy 4:42; 19:3–6. Let us now explore what Deuteronomy 19 says about what to do with someone who murders.

1. How does 19:11 describe one who murders?

   ____

   ____

2. If one is proven to have murdered, what is to happen to him in the City of Refuge? (19:12–13)

   ____

   ____

3. Why do you think 19:14 speaks about removing a boundary mark in the context of the Cities of Refuge?

   ____

   ____

A biblical trial must be conducted to determine if what was done was premeditated murder or an accident. Conducting such a trial is described in 19:15–21.

4. How many witnesses are necessary to convict someone of murder?

____

5. What important procedure in a court must be done according to
   19:16–18?

____

6. What is the penalty for a false witness? (19:19)

____

____

Excursus:
Lex Talionis (The Law of Talion)[12]

Deuteronomy 19:21 and a parallel passage in Exodus 21:18–25 are classic expressions of what is called Lex Talionis (The Law of Talion, or "Law of Retaliation"). This legal expression has to do with the law of retaliation, whereby a punishment resembles the offense committed in kind and degree. The Law of Talion is usually understood to mean identical physical retaliation is given for physical injury suffered. The idea is that when a serious injury or even a death comes inadvertently from one's negligence or carelessness, the guilty one is required to suffer the same fate. From this it would seem that if someone lost an arm, the perpetrator's arm should be cut off, or if the victim lost an ear, then the violator's ear should be removed. This principle is based on the passages that say, "eye for eye, tooth for tooth, hand for hand, foot for foot, burn for burn, wound for wound, bruise for bruise ". (Exodus 21:24–25)

However, does a literal interpretation do justice to these passages? We think that the Torah should be understood differently. In both passages, the language of the Torah is worded so that it reads that the criminal "gives" to the victim something in payment for what has been done. The Torah states the principle for such giving by using the verses quoted above (Exodus 21:24–25). However, were the Torah's intention to *extract* an eye from the villain, the use of the word "give" is inappropriate. The *lex talionis* punishment is meant to take from the guilty, not to *give* to the victim. Certainly, the victim has no desire to

____

[12] The following material is taken from *Exodus: Briteinu Torah Commentary*, to be published in 2022 by Shoreshim Publishing and by the author.

receive a gouged-out eye. It should have said, "and you shall *take* eye for eye..." On the contrary, giving is something meant to reach the recipient.

Two examples from the text will suffice to show that monetary compensation fits the passages in question, rather than handing over a dismembered limb. The first example is in Exodus 21:18–19. Here we see a case where there is wilful harm done to someone which does not result in death. In the English world, we would call this "assault and battery". The recompense in such a case is that the perpetrator must *pay* for the victim's loss of time at work and medical expenses.

A second example follows in Exodus 21:22–25. Here, two men are fighting and a pregnant woman, who is an innocent bystander, perhaps a wife, who might be attempting to stop the fight, accidentally gets hurt and loses an unborn baby in the process, but she herself is unhurt. The recompense here is that the perpetrator must *pay* whatever the judges dictate. However, the principle for the judges' decision concerning what the recompense would be is stated in Exodus 21:23 and 25: "But if there is serious injury, you are to take life for life, eye for eye, tooth for tooth, hand for hand, foot for foot, burn for burn, wound for wound, bruise for bruise."

In this light, our passages both in Exodus and Deuteronomy indicate to us that *monetary* value and not physical compensation was, indeed, the intent of Torah. In the first example above (Exodus 21:22), the text says that the guilty one simply, "shall pay". Exodus 21: 28–32 speaks of cases where an ox gores people, even after the owner of that bull had been made aware that this had happened before. In this case, although death was accidental, the owner was sentenced to death as he had not heeded the previous warnings. (Exodus 21:29). It would seem perfectly just for the owner to be put to death also, as the Torah states in Exodus 21:29. However, Exodus 21:30 says that it was possible for the guilty owner to redeem his life, that is purchase his life back by payment of a ransom, that is, money.

Thus, the law of talion is usually understood to mean identical physical injury inflicted in retaliation for physical injury suffered. The idea is that when a serious injury or even a death comes inadvertently from one's negligence or carelessness, instead of requiring the guilty one to suffer the same fate, he/she is permitted to redeem his life by paying a just fee determined by the courts of the holy community.

Holy Military: Chapter 20

The military is the final governmental institution Deuteronomy discusses. To some, it seems strange that God would sanction the military. The thinking is that God is a God who loves and makes peace — which is true. However, He is also holy. God told Abraham in Genesis 15:16 that Abraham's descendants will go down to Egypt; but then the Lord would bring them up out of servitude to live in the Promised Land. For that to happen, they would have to dispossess the inhabitants. However, God told Israel that He would use them as a tool of judgement for the sin of the inhabitants of the Land, the Canaanites/Amorites. He said, "Then in the fourth generation they will return here [the Land of Canaan], for the iniquity of the Amorite is not yet complete." This, then, is the main reason God was giving instructions about an army. Israel would have to defeat the inhabitants of Canaan on the battlefield to take their inheritance by God's promise.

1. What frame of mind does God instruct Israel to have as they face war in the Land? (20:1)

   Why can they feel/think that way? (20:1–4)

2. When Israel went into battle, who was to speak to the army first?

   a. Why do you think God instructed them to do so?

   b. What were they to say?

3. According to 20:5, besides the priests, who else was to address the army before battle?

4. In 20:5–8, what four things would prohibit a man from serving in the army?

a ____

b ____

c ____

d ____

5. What was to be said to the enemy before a battle begins? (20:10–11)

____

____

6. According to 20:11, If the city agrees to peace, what was to happen to the inhabitants?

____

____

7. If the city does not agree to peace, what was to happen to the inhabitants? (20:12–14)

____

____

8. Why do you think there is a difference between how cities that were near to Israel were to be treated differently than cities that were not close to Israel? (See 20:10–15; 20:16–18.)

____

____

9. What reason does 20:18 give about why such a harsh treatment of cities living close to Israel? See the comments in the box on the next page.

____

____

10. What does 20:19–20 say about what Israel was to do with trees in a battle? Why do you think it says that?

____

____

According to Deuteronomy 20:18, the aim of this harsh policy is to prevent Israel from being influenced by the Canaanites to adopt their abhorrent practices. The Torah regards preventing such influence as a matter of life and death since it teaches that Israel's security depends on exclusive loyalty to the Lord and eschewing Canaanite abominations (Deuteronomy 4:26; 7:4; 11:13–21). It views Israel as a small, impressionable nation living in a pagan world, with a record of susceptibility to the lure of paganism that made stringent precautions necessary (see Exodus 32 and Numbers 25:1–3). In Deuteronomy, the Canaanites' guilt in practicing child sacrifice—that is, ritual murder—underscored the necessity of forestalling their influence and eliminated any doubt that they deserved annihilation. The frequency with which enemy populations were annihilated in the ancient world made this seem an acceptable way of eliminating the danger. The basis of this policy is not ethnic, but behavioral; Deuteronomy 13:16 requires that Israelite cities that lapse into paganism be treated the same way.

JPS Torah Commentary: Deuteronomy
~ Jeffrey F. Tigay, p. 189 ~

From this point on until the end of the Covenant Responsibilities section at 26:19, Deuteronomy deals with many individual issues related to daily life in the Land. It is difficult to find a context for all of the subject, other than the fact that they are all part of what one might encounter during the natural course of his/her life.

Unknown Murder/Death: 21:1–9

Sometimes people might encounter someone who is killed without knowing how it happened or, if it is purposeful, who the perpetrator is. This is the issue in 21:1–9

1. Who is to take immediate responsibility for the case? (21:2–3)

2. What are the different elements to the ritual described in 21:4–7?

3. How does 21:8 describe the expiatory character of this ritual?

Because of its puzzling elements, rabbinic texts list this ceremony, along with the goat sent to Azazel on the Day of Atonement and the red heifer (Leviticus 16; Numbers 19), among the commandments for which there is no apparent reason and which other nations and the impulse for evil challenge. Rabbinic sources report that the ceremony was abolished in the first century CE because murder had become common and was committed openly; even if the authorities did not know who the killer was, it was highly unlikely that nobody knew, as verse 1 requires.

JPS Torah Commentary: Deuteronomy

4. Given what we previously studied about some of the functions of the priests, why do you think the priests are called on the scene of the death? (21:5)

5. What do you think was symbolized by the elders of the city washing their hands in front of the priests? (21:6)

6. What seems to be the whole point of doing this ritual for an unsolved murder? What might this teach us about the value of life in the Holy Community?

Family Relationships: 21:10–21

This next section deals with various relationships within the family. These are unusual situations, but nevertheless, the type of things one does/did encounter in daily family life.

1. What was an Israelite to do when he found a woman that he wanted to take for a wife who was taken in battle, and he wanted to have her for a wife? (21:10–14)

2. What was this woman to do? (21:13)

All of this apparently was a sign that she was to leave her old life and become part of life as an Israelite.

3. What was the man instructed to do if this woman displeased him and he did not want to marry her? (21:14)

4. What was to be his attitude towards her and how this was then
   reflected in how he was to treat her? (21:14)

____

____

Multiple Wives: 21:15–17

1. What are your thoughts about the fact that Deuteronomy does not
   seem to instruct the Israelites to have only one wife? (21:15)

____

____

2. Where in the Torah would we find instructions about having one
   wife and/one husband?

____

3. What does 21:15–17 teach about what to do with the firstborn son
   when two wives are involved?

____

____

> The terms *love* and *hate* (*dislike*) in the context of polygamous
> marriage may not connote the clear distinction that is implied in
> English. The difference may range from the extremes of "love"
> and "hate" to the contrast between 'more loved' and 'less loved'
> (though not 'hated'), i.e. one wife was preferred to the other
> **Tyndale Old Testament Commentary**
> **~ J. A. Thompson, p. 251 ~**

Troubled Children: 21:18–21

Many families have children that are sometimes very difficult to handle.
It does not always reflect on the parents. In other words, just because a
child is unruly does not mean that it is because the parents did not raise
him/her properly. Children are children and everyone is different. The
Torah in this section teaches parents what to do if there is truly a child
with a severe discipline problem.

1. According to 21:18 and 20, what are the characteristics of the kind of troubled child which requires special handling?

2. What should parents do first if they have such a child? (21:18)

3. If the first step does not work and the child persists in stubbornness and rebellion, what is to be done next? (21:19–20)

4. What is the final step in dealing with a child who is:
   - Stubborn
   - Rebellious
   - Will not listen to his father or his mother
   - Will not listen to the elders
   - Is a glutton
   - Is a drunkard?

Like all other times when someone is put to death, it is understood that there must be proper judicial procedure such as witnesses and an investigation, as explained in 21:21-23

> Executing a son has been a very rare experience among Israelites. We have no examples (that we know about) from ancient Israel. We may have here another example of a penalty stated in an extreme form in order to underline the serious nature of the crime.
>
> "The Talmud cites this passage as the basis of the requirement that all persons must be buried on the day of their death unless a delay is necessary for a suitably honorable burial."
>
> **Jeffrey H. Tigay, *Deuteronomy*, (JPS), 198**

5. What does 21:21 say about the purpose for such a severe
    punishment?

____

____

6. What should be done to a corpse if the criminal is to be hung on a tree?
   (21:22–23)

____

> The Hebrew word translated "curse" in 21:23 is the word *kelalah*
> (קללה). It has to do with treating something or someone as if they
> do not matter very much, treating lightly.
>
> The meaning of "under God's curse" (21:23) has long been
> debated. Since judgment basically is God's, the judgment that takes
> a person's life out of the covenant community as a perpetrator of
> the worst kind of sin (*het'* "capital offense") and displays that
> judgment by the humiliation of hanging his body in public shows
> that that person is under God's curse. Paul's citation of this verse to
> illustrate the extent of Yeshua's humiliation on the cross as a curse
> of one exposed as a criminal — though he was bearing the sins of
> others — is very apt (Galatians 3:13).
>
> **Earl S. Kalland, *Deuteronomy:***
> ***The Expositor's Bible Commentary*, comments on Dt. 21:23**

Consideration to Others: 22:1–8

The first eight verses of chapter 22 speak about showing consideration
to other in doing practical acts of kindness for their good.

1. According to 22:1–3, what does the Torah teach about "anything
    lost by your countryman, which he has lost, and you have found"?

____

____

2. Give some examples that the Torah cites.

____

____

____

The Mixtures 22:9–11

1. 22:9–11 seems rather unconnected. However, what, in fact, do these verses have in common?

____

____

> The prohibitions include *what we eat* (two kinds of seeds), *what we wear* (two kinds of materials), *and how we work* (two kinds of animals). These are the basic things of life, things we do every day. Hence, we suggest that these things are teaching tools about everyday life.

2. Perhaps these instructions against mixtures might serve as reminding tools that we, in fact, as believers in Yeshua are not mixtures. Look up the following passages and see if you can discover what they say about our core being in Yeshua. In other words, what do they say about us not being a "mixture"?

   a. **Romans 5:19** | "For as through the one man's disobedience the many were made sinners, even so through the obedience of the One the many will be made righteous."

   ____

   b. **2 Corinthians 5:21** | "He made Him who knew no sin *to be* sin on our behalf, so that we might become the righteousness of God in Him."

   ____

   c. **2 Corinthians 5:17** | "Therefore if anyone is in Messiah, *he is* a new creature; the old things passed away; behold, new things have come."

   ____

   d. **Romans 7:17** | "So now, no longer am I the one doing it, but sin which dwells in me."

____

____

____

e. **Romans 6:4, 6** | "Therefore we have been buried with Him through baptism [union with] into death, so that as Messiah was raised from the dead through the glory of the Father, so we too might walk in newness of life….knowing this, that our old self was crucified with *Him,* in order that our body of sin might be done away with, so that we would no longer be slaves to sin…"

The Exclusions   23:1–3, 7

According to 23:1–3, 7 certain people are to be excluded from participation in God's House.

1. Who are these people?

    a. ____

    b. ____

    c. ____

2. Why do you think they are to be excluded? What does the text say, if anything?

3. We can think of at least two biblical examples of exceptions to these instructions. Look up the following verses and see if you can determine
    a. What nationality were these people?
    b. What is it that makes them exceptions? What do they have in common that will make all who are in their situation exceptions also?

    Example #1 — Joshua 2:1–13

    Example #2 — Ruth 1:15–18

The rest of chapter 23 to the end of 26:15 speaks of various ways that the community of Israelites were to maintain community purity. A variety of topics is mentioned.

1. What kind of purity does 23:9–14 discuss?

____

____

2. How were Israelites to treat runaway slaves? (23:15–16)

____

____

> Note: In 23:17 where the text speaks about cult prostitutes, the Hebrew refers to such as a *kadesh* (קדש). This Hebrew word groups usually refers to holiness. By the use here (and other places) we can see that holiness really means to be set apart. It does not refer to any intrinsic morality, as the Hebrew word is used in reference to a cult prostitute. This parallels its use in other ancient Semitic languages.

3. What does 23:19–20 say about borrowing money from other Israelites?

____

____

4. 23:21–23 teach about making vows. What do these verses say about making vows and why do you think it is important?

____

____

The whole issue of making a vow is one of integrity. No one is required to do it. It is voluntary. Are we a person of our word or not? God wants us to think seriously what we say and what we promise. Otherwise, we cannot be trusted.

5. 23:24–25 teach about the procedure that is called "gleaning."
   According to these verses how can one glean from a farmer's field?

Divorce and Re-Marriage   24:1–5

The important subject of divorce and remarriage is mentioned in 24:1–
5. The following questions deal with some of the most important
aspects of this passage.

1. According to 24:1 what is to be done if someone wanted to divorce
   their spouse?

2. What is the condition for the divorce, according to 24:1?

3. According to 24:2 is the spouse permitted to marry someone else?
   Give the evidence.

4. What do 24:3–4 teach about what happens if the second spouse
   divorces and she desires to go back to the first spouse?

   What is the reason given for this in 24:4?

"The issue here is not divorce and its grounds *per se* but prohibition of
remarriage to a mate whom one has previously divorced."[13] Moreover,
"had she not remarried, there would be no objection to the couple's
reunion."[14]

---

[13] The NET Bible, Second Edition Notes (NET Notes), note on Deuteronomy
24:4

[14] Tigay, *op. cit*, 222.

5 If the teaching in 24:1–3 is not heeded, what are some of the effects, according to 24:4?

____

____

6. What is one final instruction about marriage found in 24:5?

____

____

Why do you think this teaching is a wise one?

____

This pattern of teaching by loosely connected assorted topics continues through chapters 24 to the middle of chapter 26. After each reference below, list the topic that passage mentions and then seek to ascertain the wisdom of its teaching. Sometime the verses say it specifically, other times we will have to think more about it.

24:6, 10–13
a. What do these verses teach?

____

b. The Wisdom for the Teaching

____

____

24:7
a. What do these verses teach?

____

b. The Wisdom for the Teaching

____

____

24:8–9
a. What do these verses teach?

____

b. The Wisdom for the Teaching

____

____

24:14–15; 25:4
a. What do these verses teach?

b. The Wisdom for the Teaching

24:16–18; 25:1–3
a. What do these verses teach?

b. The Wisdom for the Teaching

24:19–17, 22
a. What do these verses teach?

b. The Wisdom for the Teaching

25:5–10
a. What do these verses teach?

b. The Wisdom for the Teaching

25:11–12
a. What do these verses teach?

b. The Wisdom for the Teaching

25:13–16

a. What do these verses teach?

____

b. The Wisdom for the Teaching

____

____

25:17–19

a. What do these verses teach?

____

b. The Wisdom for the Teaching

____

____

26:1–15

a. What do these verses teach?

____

b. The Wisdom for the Teaching

____

____

COVENANT RENEWAL RATIFICATION   26:16–19

The long section containing the covenant responsibilities comes to a close at 26:15. Moshe clarified to the Israelites what their personal and national lives would look like if they agreed to renew the Mt. Sinai Covenant. We will begin, therefore, at 26:16 in our third and final book in the Studies in Deuteronomy.

SOURCES USED IN DEUTERONOMY

Aharoni, Yohanan. *The Land of the Bible: A Historical Geography.* Philadelphia: Westminster Press, 1979.

Archer, Gleason L., Jr. *A Survey of Old Testament Introduction.* Chicago: Moody Press, 1964.

Berkowitz, Ariel & D'vorah. *Torah Rediscovered.* Richmond, MI: Shoreshim Publishing, 2012.

Bolen, Todd. *Pictorial Library of Bible Lands*, 4 CDs of original photographs, categorized and labelled, 2000. (See: www.bibleplaces.com).

Bolen, Todd and Schlegel, Bill. *The Geography of Transjordan —* Unpublished Field Study Notes prepared for use in "Transjordan," a historical geography course taught by the authors as part of the Israel-Bible-Extension Campus of the Master's University ("IBEX").

Bonchek, Avigdor. *Studying the Torah: A Guide to In-Depth Interpretation.* Northvale, NJ: Jason Aronson, 1996.

Cardozo, Nathan T. Lopes. *The Written and Oral Torah: A Comprehensive Introduction.* Northvale, NJ: Jason Aronson, Inc., 1997.

Craige, Peter C. *The Book of Deuteronomy* (*New International Commentary on the Old Testament*). Grand Rapids, Eerdmans, 1976.

Gaebelein, Frank E. *The Expositor's Bible Commentary*, Vol. 1. Grand Rapids: Zondervan, 1979.

Glueck, Nelson. *The River Jordan: Being an Illustrated Account of Earth's Most Sacred River.* Philadelphia: The Westminster Press, 1946.

Goldberg, Louis. *Deuteronomy: Bible Study Commentary.* Grand Rapids: Zondervan, 1986.

Harrison, R. K. *Introduction to the Old Testament.* Grand Rapids: Eerdmans, 1969, 1991.

Har-El, Menashe, *Understanding the Creation.* Jerusalem: Carta, 2018. (Note: The title is deceptive. This is not an exposition of Genesis chapter 1. It is a book about the geographical features of the Land of Israel, particularly the geology and flora of the Land.).

Hareuveni, Nogah. *Desert and Shepherd in Our Biblical Heritage.* Neot Kedumim: The Biblical Landscape Reserve in Israel, 1991.

Hertz, J. H. *The Pentateuch and Haftarahs.* 2nd ed. London: Soncino Press, 1987.

Finegan, Jack. *Light from the Ancient Past,* vol. 1. Princeton: Princeton University Press, 1959.

Hoerth, Alfred J., Mattingly, Gerald L., and Yamauchi, Edwin M. eds. *The Peoples of the Old Testament World.* Grand Rapids: Baker Book House, 1994.

Keil, C.F. and Delitzsch, F. *Commentary on the Old Testament,* 10 vols. Grand Rapids: Eerdmans, 1973 reprint.

Kline, Meredith G. *The Structure of Biblical Authority.* Grand Rapids: Eerdmans, 1972.

———. *Treaty of the Great King: The Covenant Structure of Deuteronomy.* Grand Rapids: Eerdmans, 1963.

Leibowitz, Nechama. *Studies in the Weekly Sidra,* 7 vols. Jerusalem: Eliner Library, The World Zionist Organization, 1993.

Munk, Elie. *The Call of the Torah,* 5 vols. Translated by E.S. Mazer. Brooklyn, NY: Mesorah Publications, 1992.

Merrill, Eugene H. *Kingdom of Priests: A History of Old Testament Israel.* Grand Rapids: Baker, 1996.

Rosenbaum, M. and Silbermann, A. M. trans. *Pentateuch with Targum Onkelos, Haphtarot, and Rashi's Commentary: Deuteronomy.* New York: Hebrew Publishing Co, ND.

Thompson, J. A. *Deuteronomy* (TOTC). (Leicester, UK: InterVarsity Press, 1974.

Tigay, Jeffery H. *The JPS Bible Commentary: Haftarot.* Philadelphia: The Jewish Publication Society, 1996.

Walton, John H.; Matthews, Victor H.: and Chavalas, Mark W. *The IVP Bible Background Commentary: Old Testament.* Downers Grove: InterVarsity Press, 2000.

ICTIONARIES, ENCYCLOPEDIAS, BIBLE ATLASES

Accordance 7.1. OakTree Software, 2006. This electronic resource includes a host of materials we used for Briteinu including Bibles, Bible Atlas, Biblical Archaeology Review pictures, and much more. Contact www.accordancebible.com

Aharoni, Yohanan; Avi-Yona, Michael; Rainey, Anson F.; and Safrai, Ze'ev. *The Macmillan Bible Atlas*, Completely Revised Third Edition. New York: Simon & Schuster Macmillan Company and Jerusalem: Carta, 1993.

Bromiley, Geoffrey W. gen. ed. *The International Standard Bible Encyclopedia*, 4 vols. Grand Rapids: Eerdmans, 1979.

Brown, Francis, Driver, S. R., and Briggs, Charles A. The New Brown, Driver, Briggs, *Gesenius Hebrew and English Lexicon*. Peabody, MA: Hendrickson Publishers, 1979.

Freedman, David Noel, Editor-in-Chief. *Eerdmans Dictionary of the Bible*. Grand Rapids: Eerdmans, 2000.

Jenni, Ernst and Westermann, Claus *Theological Lexicon of the Old Testament*. Peabody, MA: Hendrickson, 1997.

Koehler, L. and Baumgartner, W., eds. *Hebrew and Aramaic Lexicon of the Old Testament (Unabridged 2-Volume Study Edition)*. 2 vols.; trans. M. E. J. Richardson. Leiden & Boston: Brill, 2002.

Rainey, Anson and Notley, R. Stephen. *The Sacred Bridge*. Carta: Jerusalem, 2006.

Schlegel, William. *Satellite Bible Atlas: Historical Geography of the Bible*, 2013. schlegel4@gmail.com

Helpful Websites

www.biblearchaeology.org/
A website of the Associates for Biblical Research, an excellent source for information about archaeology from an evangelical point of view. The home of *Bible and Spade* magazine.

www.biblicalarchaeology.org/
This is the home of the popular magazine called *Biblical Archaeology Review*.

www.BiblePlaces.com
An important source for pictures of biblical sites and culture, both in Israel and in the Mediterranean world in general.

www.TorahResource.com

www.TorahResourcesInternational.com

www.torahtruths.com

OTHER BOOKS BY ARIEL & D'VORAH BERKOWITZ
(Alphabetical Order)

A Week in the Life of the Lamb

*Celebrating Shabbat in the Home
of the Redeemed (In Progress)*

Foundations Rediscovered (online course)

Hanukkah in the Home of the Redeemed

"Open My Eyes" (גל עיני)
Studying & Teaching the Bible Made Simple

*Studies in the Book of Deuteronomy: Renewing the Covenant
Books 1 , 2, & 3*

*Studies in the Book of Joshua:
The Covenants in Action*

Take Hold

*The Briteinu Torah Commentary:
Vol. 1— Bereshit: The Foundations of Covenant
Vol. 2— Shemot: The Written Covenant
(In Progress)*

*The Torah of the Sages:
A Simple Introduction to the Oral Torah*

The Twelve Overlooked Prophets

Torah Rediscovered

MBTA: Modular Biblical Training Academy
The Academy offers Biblical training as a unique place of
learning for all ages. The style of learning helps to develop a
Biblical vocabulary and build fundamental concepts needed for
learning Torah.

To order any of these books, please see our website:
www.torahresourcesinternational.com

ABOUT THE AUTHOR

Ariel Berkowitz holds a B.S. from West Chester State University and Philadelphia Biblical University (PBU) together, an M. Div. Biblical Theological Seminary, and attended classes at Rodef Torah School of Jewish Studies. D'vorah studied social work at West Chester and PBU. Both of them are instructors with Torah Resources International. Ariel has been a full-time instructor at Israel College of Bible (early 1990's) and is presently an Adjunct Professor (since 1995), with "IBEX" the Israeli campus of The Master's University. He is also an Instructor with TorahResource Institute. D'vorah is the developer and instructor of MBTI (Modular Biblical Training Institute. Ariel and D'vorah have four grown children and seven grandchildren. They live in the Negev, Israel.

www.ingramcontent.com/pod-product-compliance
Lightning Source LLC
Chambersburg PA
CBHW060911130726
48001CB00006B/2190